T0064491

My Brother Has Sickle Cell

Written by
Dr. Erica D. Gamble
and
Dwayne C. Robinson

Illustrated by
Rebekah Crowmer

AuthorHouse™ LLC
1663 Liberty Drive
Bloomington, IN 47403
www.authorhouse.com
Phone: 1-800-839-8640

© 2014 Dr. Erica D. Gamble. All Rights Reserved.

No part of this book may be reproduced, stored in a retrieval system,
or transmitted by any means without the written permission of the author.

Published by AuthorHouse 03/13/2014

ISBN: 978-1-4918-6929-1 (sc)
978-1-4918-6930-7 (e)

Library of Congress Control Number: 2014904352

Any people depicted in stock imagery provided by Thinkstock are models,
and such images are being used for illustrative purposes only.
Certain stock imagery © Thinkstock.

This book is printed on acid-free paper.

Because of the dynamic nature of the Internet, any web addresses or links contained in this
book may have changed since publication and may no longer be valid. The views expressed
in this work are solely those of the author and do not necessarily reflect the views of
the publisher, and the publisher hereby disclaims any responsibility for them.

authorHOUSE®

My brother Alvin and I are only 2 years apart. We share lots of things- same mom, same dad, how much we love basketball, football, our dog Diamond and video games.

Charles loves his brother Alvin. He looks up to him in many ways. Alvin is great at so many things-swimming, playing basketball, and playing musical instruments. Sometimes Alvin gets very sick, he has pain in his body and sometimes cannot walk. He cries out because he hurts and it makes me feel sad. What is happening to Alvin?

After Alvin gets his medicine or after he returns from his visit to the hospital he gets back to his normal self-laughing, playing games, having fun and being big brother. Alvin is my big brother. He is strong he is brave but he has a disease called sickle cell.

In this genuine and emotional story, told from a brother's point of view, we meet a family whose oldest son teaches them the importance of love, hope, tolerance and strength.

Dr. Erica Gamble, professor, author, life-coach. Mother and wife has paired with her son Dwayne to co-author this uplifting book based on their personal perspectives and experiences with Aaron, Erica's son and Dwayne's brother who has sickle cell anemia.

Alvin and I look a lot alike. We both have brown skin, big brown eyes and funny shaped noses.

Alvin and I may look alike but we are not alike. We like some of the same things-

Our dog Diamond

How much we love Oreo cookies

Playing in the backyard

Swimming

Football

Basketball and

Trains

I like being Alvin's younger brother. Being brothers does not mean that we are the same. I am 2 years younger, I love cars and baseball cards and I have lots of friends.

Alvin is skinnier than me, he is taller than me, and he can't seem to sit still-but when Alvin is not feeling well he gets very quiet, sits alone and will take long naps. Alvin has the biggest smile in the world- I like to call him smiley!

3

I always like being happy, chasing lightening bugs, reading comic books with my granny and playing Uno.

But Alvin is different, his eyes are yellow at times, he might cry a lot, and always seems sad. He sticks really close to mommy- he never wants to leave her side.

Mommy seemed really worried about Alvin. She spent a lot of time taking him to the doctor and giving him medicine. He was always in pain and hurting-I knew something was wrong.

Mommy wanted me to understand why Alvin cried
a lot and seemed sad many days. There were many
days and nights that Alvin had to stay in the
hospital- mommy stayed with him too.

That made me sad..to see Alvin this way.

It was hard for Alvin to play for long periods of time with me or other kids. He never could tell us how he really felt. That made mommy sad but she always treated Alvin normal and wanted him to fit in.

When Alvin wanted to do something he learned to give it his all. Even when he was not feeling well. Sometimes it was hard to be Alvin's younger brother. When he is feeling good he smiles hard and he beats me at everything- every game, every race, everything. Other times it can be hard because Alvin is in pain, feeling sad in the hospital.

There are times when I wish I could trade places with Alvin, go to the doctor for him, miss school for him and take his medicine for him. I know that Alvin would love to trade places with me too- making friends, playing sports in school and not in pain.

There are many days when Alvin is happy, not in the hospital, playing and smiling and going places with mommy, and I. He goes many days without being sick.

There are other times when Alvin will be gone in the hospital for many days. After Alvin's last hospital stay mommy came home crying. I asked mommy "what's wrong"? "Is Alvin ok"?

Mommy said, "Alvin has sickle cell"!

Sickle cell? Alvin's doctor sat down with mommy and I to explain what sickle is.

Have you ever seen a sickle? It's a farm tool with a curved, sharp edge for cutting wheat. Sickle cell anemia is a disease of the blood. It gets its name because a person's red blood cells are shaped like sickles, or crescent moons, instead of their usual round, disc shape.

When red blood cells are shaped like sickles or crescent moons, they can get stuck, especially inside smaller blood vessels. This keeps blood from flowing properly in the body, which can cause a lot of pain, especially in the bones. Important organs like the brain, heart, and kidneys need constant blood flow to work properly.

Sickle Cell   Normal Red Blood Cell

After learning what sickle cell is I now know more about my brother. Alvin is special and he has a special love for animals, especially Diamond. When Alvin and Diamond are together it helps to ease his pain. Diamond make's Alvin feel better- she licks his face, plays catch with him, lays on his leg when he is in pain and stays close to him when he is sad. Only Alvin can get Diamond to sit run or roll over.

Alvin has special ways that he likes to deal with his pain. Playing basketball in the backyard. He likes to show off his Boy Scout badges, his new colorful sneakers, and how well he can play the piano.

Alvin can be mean when he does not feel good. I know that my brother loves me and really does not want me to be sad. But when I am in pain or feeling sick, he makes me feel better-he does not want me to hurt like him.

Alvin has made me a better younger brother, he has taught me to be strong and how to love and be strong no matter what he is going through Alvin is God's child and he made him special- special with sickle cell to help others.

Alvin has sickle cell but sickle cell does not have Alvin. Anyone who knows my brother knows he is the coolest kid with the biggest heart and the biggest smile. He is always helpful and really knows how to be a big brother.

I am blessed to be Alvin's brother and to have someone to share my life with. I look forward to seeing Alvin smile each and every day-his smile lights up my world.

Some common symptoms of sickle cell anemia

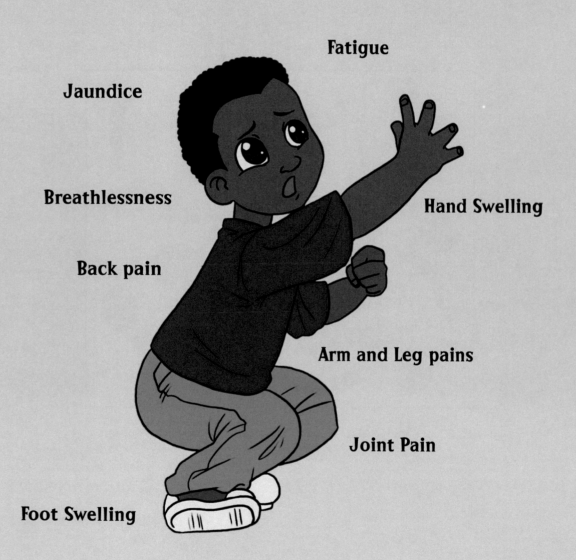

Fatigue

Jaundice

Breathlessness

Hand Swelling

Back pain

Arm and Leg pains

Joint Pain

Foot Swelling

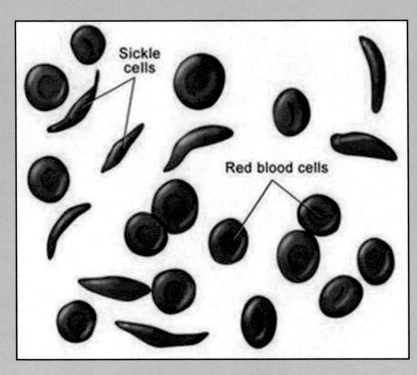

Sickle cells (Drepanocytes)

Why we wrote this book-how it could help you!

We offer this book as a gift to families struggling with sickle cell disease and to those who have no sickle cell in their immediate families but who have friends facing it. My brother has sickle cell is a book about a disease that many children face but often do not talk about. It also may help siblings to understand what their brother or sister might be dealing with. This book was a much-needed inspiration.

Dr. Erica Gamble

My oldest son Aaron was diagnosed at birth with sickle cell disease. As a young, new mother I had no knowledge of this disease nor the impact that it would have on my child's life. I was told that the life expectancy for my child would be around the age of 17-especially since there is currently no cure. Although my son is currently 23, I have remained optimistic throughout his entire life and thank God that he has lived a fairly normal life to date. Today, recent research, treatments and improved medical procedures have helped to prolong the life of patients with this disease. Future treatments may involve genetic engineering where cures might be achieved.

About Sickle Cell Anemia: When a child inherits two substitution beta globin genes (the sickle cell gene) from both parents, the child has Sickle Cell Anemia (SS). Individuals with sickle cell anemia may acquire symptoms of sickle cell disease. Populations that have a high frequency of sickle cell anemia are those of African and Indian descents. In the United States, the disease most commonly affects African-Americans.

When sickle-shaped red blood cells get stuck in blood vessels this can cause episodes of pain called crises. Other symptoms include: delayed growth, strokes, and jaundice (yellowish hue to the skin and eyes because of liver damage).

In the United States with an estimated population of over 270 million about 1,000 babies are born with sickle cell disease each year. Approximately 70,000-100,000 individuals in the United States have this disease and 3 million have the trait.

Dwayne Robinson

I love my brother Aaron- he is certainly my inspiration. My goal of this book is to be able to help another younger brother whose older brother has sickle cell truly understand what the impact can be like. I feel that there is a huge stigma associated with this disease and people should educate themselves to gain a better understanding. Sickle cell is not contagious and people who have this disease are normal- they just might require support and prayer during their times of crisis.

Growing up my brother never talked about his disease and never let others know that he had this illness. He was embarrassed and thought he would be judged. Today, I recognize that if you have a family member, friend or loved one with this disease it is important to support, be educated and join our efforts to STOMP sickle cell and help to find a cure.

Dr. Erica Gamble, professor, author, life-coach, mother and wife has paired with her son Dwayne to co-author this uplifting book based on their personal perspectives and experiences with Aaron, Erica's son and Dwayne's brother who has sickle cell anemia. She has been a past board member for the sickle cell anemia association and worked as an advocate and volunteer since 1993 to help families who are raising children with sickle cell. She also serves as an after school volunteer for children with sickle cell in hopes of educating and inspiring children and parents struggling with this disease. Dr. Gamble plans to start an organization in Atlanta and eventually expand globally dedicated to helping children with sickle cell gain access to affordable treatments and therapies.

Dwayne Robinson, age 20, wrote this book with his mother, Dr. Gamble, to help share awareness about sickle cell with other children from his perspective as a young boy. Dwayne has assisted his mother in volunteering with the foundation and has based narrative for this story on real events that happened in his family. Dwayne is a junior at Georgia Southern University in Statesboro Georgia and Dr. Gamble resides in Marietta, Georgia.

Aaron Robinson, age 22 is "Alvin". He is a student at Strayer University in Atlanta Georgia and continues to manage his health and work with his family to help find a cure for sickle cell.

Printed in the United States
By Bookmasters